DON'T GIVE YOURSELF AWAY, BUT TO GOD ONLY

JUANITA (AKA) KIAMOTA

WESTBOW
PRESS®
A DIVISION OF THOMAS NELSON
& ZONDERVAN

Scripture taken from the King James Version of the Bible.

WestBow Press books may be ordered through booksellers or by contacting:

WestBow Press
A Division of Thomas Nelson & Zondervan
1663 Liberty Drive
Bloomington, IN 47403
www.westbowpress.com
1 (866) 928-1240

ISBN: 978-1-5127-3810-0 (sc)

Library of Congress Control Number: 2016938699

Print information available on the last page.

WestBow Press rev. date: 4/15/2016

Contents

INTRODUCTION

I am compelled to write this story about life experiences, focusing mainly on marriage and relationships, in which men and women of faith might face in their Christian journey. Before I begin this message, I would like to first thank Almighty God for instilling in me the confidence and wisdom needed in order to complete this assignment. I thank God for His amazing awesomeness and love shown to me this day and throughout the years. My fervent prayer is, *"LET THE WORDS OF MY MOUTH AND THE MEDITATION OF MY HEART BE ACCEPTABLE IN THY SIGHT, OH LORD, MY STRENGTH AND MY REDEEMER."* **(PSALMS 19:14)**

This book is written in order that men and women of all ages and backgrounds continue to hold onto the unchanging hand of God when faced with life's challenges. These challenges are obstacles Christian men and women face when trying to remain faithful to their beliefs and to their Christian responsibilities and commitments.

I would like to mention, as well as thank, some very fine people who rendered so much to my writing of this book. These people encouraged me by praying with and for me to gain the strength and courage to believe in the power of prayer and God's magnificent love, grace and mercy.

I would like to thank my young adult children who constantly listened to me when I felt as though I wanted to quit this assignment. I thank them for encouraging me and reminding me that, I can do **ALL** things with GOD. I believe people need to be aware of the message, I believe, God has equipped me and ordained me to tell, and therefore, I realized how important it was to obey God.

I would also like to thank my long-time friends, Karen and Jimmy, who stood by me when it seemed as though the storm was raging and my task of writing this book, seemed dim. I then was reminded of God's promises, one being, "I will never leave you, neither will I ever forsake you." *(Hebrew 13:5)* It was comforting and assuring to reflect upon the promise, "Be of good courage, and He shall strengthen your heart, all ye that hope in the Lord." *(Psalm 31:24)*

I would like to thank my husband, Lenny, who always encourages me to take on new ventures. He has inspired me from the very first day, I said, "**I DO**"! I thank him also for his love and support.

I am confident that you will glean much from this book. God has said it, prepared it, and ordained it, for your reading pleasure, learning power, spiritual enlightenment and continued growth. *ENJOY and BE BLESSED!*

Chapter 1

DON'T GIVE YOURSELF AWAY- BUT TO GOD, ONLY

Don't give yourself away to anyone, but to God. When you give yourself away and the person to whom you gave yourself to decides to throw you away, and usually after some time, they do, and when the time comes to find yourself, you notice, you are lost. Symptoms of being lost are, becoming argumentative, always discontent realizing you are no longer the *"apple"* of the other person's eye, since you no longer, "rock their world, nor boat"; you no longer are given the utmost respect nor do you notice any *"real"* love or affection being given to you. You are no longer the "object of their affection". Your position of being a *"basket case"* has actually come to fruition. Now, you find yourself constantly complaining, nagging, crying, praying, and trying to figure out why you are in this particular situation and dilemma. You are at the place where no one really wants to, neither, go there with you, nor listen to your sorrowful story, nor join you in your, *"pity party"*. You find yourself all alone, believing that "God" doesn't want to hear any more of your, *"mess"*. Even though God has told you, shown you, placed people in your life for a season whom God used to help you to see the reality of things concerning your relationships, even your marital relationship, you still find yourself questioning your very existence, angry and experiencing low, self-esteem.

TASTING THE BITTERSWEET

When I was 12 years old, there were occasions when my parents would entertain friends and family on some weekend evenings. There would be fried chicken, baked ham, collard greens, macaroni and cheese casseroles, peas, rice and all kinds of deserts and beverages for the guest to eat, drink and enjoy themselves. After the guests left, my sisters and I would sneak in the living room to see what was left to eat and drink, of course, we were hoping to find soda, fired chicken, pie and cake. On one occasion, I decided to pick up this glass that I thought looked like 7 UP, took a big gulp and almost chocked to death. After experiencing an episode of coughing, choking, and what seemed as though my head was going to blow off, I was told by my mother, who came running into the living room after hearing all of the commotion, I had gulped down an alcohol beverage, known as "*Vodka*", in its purest form. I then realized it wasn't water, and it wasn't soda. In reality, it was pure liquor, which to me tasted terrible, bad, nasty, and bitter. My throat felt as though it was on fire. It was so horrible to me; it was painful going into my digestive system. That was reality! Well, one might say, I didn't know that the beverage was going to turn out to be a *bitter* drink. I didn't know that the drink was going to be painful, I just seized the opportunity to taste, not even realizing whether or not I was actually, thirsty. I thought it was going to be *sweet*. I just wanted to satisfy my desire.

When you give yourself away, you don't realize your destiny or agony. You thought by giving yourself away, the taste would be sweet and there would be nothing bitter or nasty about it, not even hurtful. To your surprise, like the tempting glass of liquid, you experience the after effects that might not be so pleasant, and now you are indeed hurting and in agony. Instead of feeling as though your head is blowing off or spinning, you are actually feeling as though you are *"losing it"* and going out of your mind, all stressed out.

ORIGIN OF SELF-ESTEEM

Self-esteem is something that is not taught in schools. It is a behavior that is developed from within. We are born with the tools to cultivate the seed that was planted in us from birth. As a synonym, the word is interchangeable and means, having a sense of pride and a realistic respect for a favorable impression of one's self. This innate, God-given attribute is lost, when we give ourselves away to anyone other than the one who gave us life. Losing confidence in self and allowing others to infuse negative energy into one's life is exactly an attack from God's enemy, the devil. Deception is an attribute of the devil. A deceiver from the very beginning of creation, the adversary tricked Eve in the Garden of Eden into believing the voice she heard was actually coming from an animal, a serpent. She was fooled due to her inexperience with life's dilemmas and had not experienced people's beguiling and deceptive ways.

Today, God's adversary is in-tuned with these modern and highly technical times. He is aware that people today, will not and do not believe that an animal has the capability to speak. However, he uses other tactics to fool and confuse God's children. These tactics, if not recognized, can either destroy you, your children, your marriage and other relationships. Attacking one's personality, self-esteem, and integrity, belittles and degrades what God has created, causing one to feel as though they are less than instead of more than or as good as. Low self-esteem can affect men, women, boys and girls, and is usually developed in the early years of one's life. Experiences that are usually caused by negativism faced by individuals, is a profound and integral fact of the onset of low self-esteem. When one is inflicted by negative people and their negative thoughts, the individual then begins to plug into the inflictor, who is usually envious, angry, and feels threatened in some way by the victim. That individual is one who possesses the seed of low self-esteem, themselves and seeks to implant it in someone's character, thus, the demise and destruction of character is ready to be birthed.

Women who marry for love and become devoted and loving wives with or without children, and love the Lord and are saved, have many envious people lurking around their husbands, children and marital situations. This is usually not realized before inviting people into their lives, and especially into their marital relationships and other affairs.

"We wrestle not against flesh and blood, but against principalities, against powers, against the rulers of the darkness of this world, against spiritual wickedness in high places." *(Ephesians 6:12)* Often times, this very fact, if not taken into consideration, due to the challenges we go through, is forgotten, and therefore, we experience stress, sickness, unhappiness, and at times, many have nervous and spiritual breakdowns instead of spiritual breakthroughs.

CAUGHT UP IN A WEB

Forsaking ourselves for the sake of "love" our lives become living sacrifices to the underserved and to those who are prone to abuse and misuse the kindness of the one who has become the *"sacrificial lamb"*. Clothed in sheep's garments and illuminating the brightness of intelligence, sex appeal and attractiveness, whether male or female, the one who loses one's self because of having the *need* to be sheltered, led and loved, is caught up by the illusory of the moment and the deceiver's *web*.

Similar to a lion, man is a hunter, always looking for his prey by any means necessary. In Roman mythology, the god, "Cupid," is always depicted as carrying a bow and arrow, whereas the bow or tubercle signified the base which must remain stable in order for the arrow to be shot in the desired direction of the object of his affection. He is often depicted as carrying two sets of arrows; one set, gold, which inspire true love, and the other, lead-headed, which inspire erotic love.

It can be noticed that *some* men of today are much like the playful Cupid who was often portrayed as a nude or sometimes diapered-winged boy or baby armed with a bow and quiver of arrows. Cupid had a flirtatious nature and often flirted with beautiful women, called Nymphs.

His playful nature of catching butterflies, throwing darts and amusing himself with adult play, prompted his mother to have to scold him for his mischievous nature.

In reflecting on the character of the mythological, "Cupid", we are reminded of husbands, wives, boyfriends, girlfriends, sister, brothers, and others who possess similar attributes and behaviorisms. Some men and women are by nature playful hunters and will shoot their affections towards those whom they are attracted to. Men and women, Christians not excluded, become attracted and distracted easily by individuals who exhibit the qualities and characteristics of those who might lack good moral judgment and possess callus personalities. These people are cunning, envious, self-centered Godless workers of witchcraft and iniquity. This observation might seem somewhat cold, and unbelievable, but in reality, are *real* and *does* exist.

Passive people are prone to keeping their eyes closed to many issues, especially to evilness, being similar to the first woman, "Eve's naivety. Their *passiveness* and *emotionalism* gets in the way of reality, and often times, they are regarded as being, *"blind"*, *"dumb"*; looking at the world through *rose-colored* glasses. They are labeled as all sorts of derogatory and demeaning adjectives. Due to their compassionate and humble personalities, many are referred to as being, "too good, too Godly, to meek and lowly". *(Galatians 5:22, 23)* They are also thought of as being, "weak".

Chapter 2

MEEKNESS VS. WEAKNESS

Meekness is one of the fruits of the Spirt and is a quality in which we must possess if we allow ourselves to be led by the spirit of God. Men and women, who have given themselves away, are mocked and scorned by others. It is good to be Godly, meek and humble because Jesus said, *"Unless we become as little children, humble, we cannot inherit the Kingdom of God."* (Matthew 18:3)

When others mock and say all sorts of evil things against you because of your meekness and humbleness, they confuse the act of being meek and humble with that of being weak and powerless. They fail to realize that the meek person is not self-willed, not continually concerned with self or his own ways, ideas, and wishes. They are willing to put themselves in second place and submit themselves to achieving what is good for others.

Meekness is the opposite of self-will, self-interest, and self-assertiveness. These qualities do not signify weakness of character, as some may think and treat you as though they do, but, it signifies *strength* of *character*, because it requires great self-control to submit to others. Therefore, when remarks are made such as, "you are too good, and I'm glad I'm not you", just know that what they are actually indicating is, the fact that they are not strong-minded and they lack Christ-like attributes. Giving yourself away to "God, only", signifies giving yourself to GOD (submitting your body, mind and soul), and letting HIM use you to HIS glory. This meekness is an attitude of heart, intertwined with your inner self and the unfading beauty of a *gentle* and *quiet spirit*, which is of great worth in GOD's sight. (1 Peter 3:4)

If you have these qualities, and no doubt you do, feel honored and know that you are God's child and HE has blessed you with a gift that many desire. The bible teaches that we should not be yoked with people who are of unlike faith and beliefs. This does not mean that we should take the statement casually and feel that even if you do become yoked with someone who does not believe in God or a higher power that he or she will change over time, because of you. Do not think that because of your beliefs, your love for them will cause them to desire to serve God.

Many mistakes are made when young men and women believe that because they attend church, participate in church activities, etc., that because of their good deed and love for the Lord, it's making a profound impression on their relationships, whether spousal, or others, and such behaviorism will cause them to desire to follow you. If that is the case, you are in for a rude awakening. Although the scriptures mention, concerning a marital relationship, that "because of the believer, the unbeliever will be saved because of the believing mate". Notice it says, the believer will be saved, and not "YOU" saving them. In other words, you can stop trying to change your spouse, which causes strife in your home, and start believing for a miracle instead. God is working to convert your spouse through you, but by your actions much more than by your words. In fact, God may prefer to do the work without your words, because your words might cause tension and division in the relationship or in the home. Remember, God sends the Holy Spirit to change your spouse's thinking and behavior. You can't convert your spouse, no one else but the Holy Spirit can do this, because matters of faith are unreasonable to the natural mind. *"The man without the spirit does not accept the things that come from the spirit of God, and they are foolishness to him, and he cannot understand them, because they are spiritually discerned."* *(1 Corinthians 2:14)*

GOD'S LOVE

Giving yourself to God, only, is when you will experience the life in which God would have you to live. God did not create you so you can be unhappy, poor, downhearted, unloved and to have low self-esteem. God's love is sufficient and he gives it abundantly. When we love someone, we show them this love by being kind, loving, thoughtful, helpful, respectful and supporting. Occasionally, we shower them with gifts to express our love and affection towards them. God's love is like that, too. However, God's love is unconditional. God's love is not prejudice, and most of the time, we don't deserve the love that HE gives us. We find ourselves not even returning the love or giving thanks for HIS love. Therefore, we are given underserved love, but yet, God still loves, without conditions. *"But God shows his love for us in*

*that while we were still sinners, Christ died for us."
(Romans 5:8)*

You may have formulated your own opinion of what true love is and this might have been shaped by your experiences with love. If you have had good experiences with relationships, then most likely, your thoughts of what true love is, probably looks like a bed of roses, beautifully arranged with a scent of spring freshness, newness, and sugar and spice. However, on the other hand, if you have experienced negativity with *"love"*, your picture of love might be something of pain, agony, abuse, distrust, dishonesty, and instead of being a bed of roses, you feel as though love is a bed of thorns, lies and deceitfulness. You also might relate to the song performed by the late Whitney Houston when she referred to love, *"Why Does it Hurt So Bad"?*

Those who have given themselves away, are hurting with regret and are now striving to recover, taking back that which others were allowed to steal, rob, and destroy from them. Realizing, finally, that there is no benefit in viewing the world through rose-colored glasses, but, challenging themselves to survive and live, not just merely existing. They are learning to say, **"NO"**, to pain, lies, abuse and deceit, and to say, **"YES"**, to gaining higher self-esteem, self-motivations, spirituality, and love of self, for a change. These men and women are learning to be noticeably "selfish" in a positive way, while still putting god First and family second, they are beginning to put "SELF" in their lives, as well; needlessly to say, they are 'LIKING IT, TOO"!

The greatest love one can experience is the love of God and self. We must learn to love ourselves, unconditionally, as God loves us, unconditionally. In other words, if we have a sore foot or a broken arm, for instance, we are not going to love our eyes and hate our foot or broken arm, are we? Of course, not! Those are our body parts and they belong to the same body. We might not like the idea, and who would, having a body part that is broken or does not function well? The bible speaks of *"cutting off"* a body member in order to enter eternal life. "If your hand or foot causes you to sin, cut it off and throw it away. It is better for you to enter life maimed or crippled than to have two hands or two feet and be thrown into eternal fire." (Matthew 18:7-9) Simply put, Jesus is saying that anything that causes you to sin and, therefore, negatively impacts your relationship with God, should be removed from your life. If there is something in our lives that should be plucked out or removed for the sake of pleasing God, we should seek to remove it. God loves us in spite of our iniquities, unconditionally, and if we say we love God, who lives in us, we show love of self by transforming our lives to the Will of God, and thus, becoming cognitive that the **Greatest love of all lives inside of us.**

GUARD YOUR HEART

Don't lose yourself to emotionalism, in that you lose your self-worth by lowering your standards and expectations of your character as well as your spirituality. Be very careful when you open your heart to *"love"*. The heart is a tender organ, and is very susceptible and responsive. It can be said, that the heart has a mind of its own. The heart can be very deceptive and because of this one must use the mind instead of the heart to make sound and effective decisions. *"Keep your heart with all vigilance, for from it, flow the springs of life." (Proverbs 4:23)* True love surpasses all understanding.

Chapter 3

LOVE AND EXPECTATIONS

True love is something we all desire to receive from any meaningful, personal relationship, such as a marital relationship, or a relationship where we are engaged to be married. In these relationships, commitments and certain responsibilities should be evident. In a marriage, for instance, both people are committed to one another. Love and respect is due one another along with friendship, caring, sharing and communicating. Spirituality should exist in a marriage since this aspect serves as a covering, shield and a protective rainbow that hovers over and surrounds the union in which God has ordained. In order for this union to be functional and wholesome, both parties, before entering such a union, must examine themselves as to their "compatibility". Questions and discussions between couples must be entertained. This will eliminate unknown surprises showing up in marriage which might result in breakups, separations or divorces.

With heartfelt honesty, don't be afraid to, with love, discuss concerns that might affect a long-term engagement or marriage. For instance, find out his or her views of employment situations. Are both parties expected to be employed? Where do you both want to live? How will bills be paid? Will the household maintain and adhere to a budget? If children are born into this marriage, will the wife be expected to work or stay at home? What is to be the relationship with the in-laws? Will the husband take care of the household expenses or will it be a shared responsibility? Will the bank accounts be separate or joint accounts?

There are so many concerns and decisions to be made and considered before taking a big leap into marriage. Since God is the creator of marriage, HE is concerned about how it is approached. We must remember that the adversary, the devil, came to steal, rob, and destroy. If he can destroy the family arrangement, by any means possible, he will do it and try it. That is why, when god's people of all ages, enter into a marital agreement, it must be done prayerfully, with counseling, and with a sound mind and attitude.

LOVE IS BLIND

Don't give yourself away to emotional and blind ignorance. The old saying that is still prevalent and meaningful today is, "love is blind". When a young woman or man is in love, it is evidential by the way they walk, talk and relate to the world. Everything and everybody appears to be beautiful and happy. Children seem to notice that there is a connection of love between couples as they stroll down the street or sit on the bus or train holding hands and gazing into each other's eyes. The woman pays no attention to the fact that perhaps the gentleman's ears, by no fault of his own, might be somewhat larger than average, or that his overbite might be very noticeable. He on the other hand, pays no attention to the fact that the woman might be slightly overweight or has rather large feet for a female. They are, however, in love. Thus, the saying, **"love is blind"**, is real. There is no one perfect, but, **GOD.**

FAITH

You must acquire faith which is a belief in something that is not yet seen and the evidence of something that will be seen and coming to fruition. For example, you might have a *belief* that the sun *will* shine although it may be raining or is cloudy—that's the thing unseen, but the thing unseen is the sun and your belief is that although the sun is *not* shining at the moment, due to cloudy skies, you believe that by the sun shining, it is evidence of the unseen thing. Thus that is *faith*.

We should also *walk in* faith by letting our steps carry us towards places where we would find the favor of God. There are times when we might find ourselves stepping not into our God-given destiny, but, walking in places where God is not pleased. Instead of giving ourselves to God, we allow people, places and things, lead us away from desirable and acceptable places.

Falling in love with persons who, don't have your best interest at heart, and, like Cupid, shot the arrow in your direction which was not the true love side, but the erotic side, will, unfortunately, mislead one to believe that it was true love. Similar to our first parent, Eve, many men and women fall victim to being beguiled into believing a lie.

Erotic love, unlike true love, is temporary and shallow; there is neither depth nor permanence to it. Eroticism, which is fleshly pleasures, only lasts as long as the flesh desires to be pleased, titillated and satisfied. When the flesh is fulfilled, there is nothing left. Eroticism does not affect the mind and has little effect on the heart. That is why a relationship built on eroticism is temporal. People should ask themselves these questions concerning relationships based on intimacy ad love: "Is this relationship alive because of sex or is this relationship built on other substantial things other than sex?" Is there a true bonding? Is there true caring for one another along with respect of character and person? Is there true love, friendship and partnership? Can the love or caring continue without a sexual relationship? Or does the relationship continue because of sexual activities? What percentage does sex play in the relationship? Notice, that these questions should be considered between *"married Christian couples"* as well as, *"non-married couples."*

We all should focus on those questions, since all people are tempted and have short comings. We all fall short of "God's Graces, thus, we are sinners, saved by God's Amazing Grace and His Mercy. However, I am not making points to make you feel guilty, nor am I being judgmental. I am, suggesting, however, that the vicissitudes of life, that is, the ups and downs, and life's uncertainties and challenges we encounter, considering these things before a marital relationship or an engagement to commit to a marital relationship is entered into, would result in a happier and a more fulfilling life.

REGAINING SELF-YOUR CHOICE

A wise counsel would be to avoid receiving in your spiritual mind, the acclamation that when you are doing well for someone else, or for yourself, you are made to feel that your good deeds are wrong. Receiving negative remarks that demoralize and are humiliating, damages one's self-esteem. It can be said to be true, that *"hurt people, hurt "other" people".* Their comments are usually directed toward you to cover up for their iniquities. In most cases, their guilt is based upon infidelity, low self-esteem, inadequacies and hidden envy characterized by their mundane and unhappy lives.

While going through the journey of turmoil, depression, and other negativity from a relationship, a marriage, a job situation or any other life ventures and situations, know that God sees all and is aware of your pain, joys, sorrows and dilemmas. HE is not only cognitive of your life, HE is actively aware and concerned about you and the situation, whatever it may be. God will always abide with you, even when at times, you feel as though he is not with you and do not care. Remember to abide with HIM and HE will abide with you, always.

In choosing to regain self, thus becoming acquainted once again with who you are and who you are in Christ, what steps are needed to take in order for this to be a successful and smooth transitions? First, you must recognize the fact that giving yourself away to someone or something, other than to our Heavenly Father, was not a desirable choice. You must become cognitive of "who" you are in Christ, Jesus, and realize that God wants you to be happy and blessed. You must know that your good deeds to others were not in vain. Even if you encountered a relationship, whether a marital one or an engagement, and you remained faithful, although your spouse or fiancé did not, don't blame yourself. If you were faithful to your commitment and to your vows, then know this, **God honors your faithfulness to your commitment and marital vows.**

It is also important to realize the fact that it was probably a slow, progressive move towards losing one's self. After all, you might have been engulfed with responsibilities, children, husband or partner, bills babysitters, education homemaker, nurse, mother and sometimes you might have had to be, both parents, cooking, shopping, wife, teacher, accountant, driver, etc. This list can go on and on for both men and women. Recognize, however, there might not be time to slowly regain self, or even as some people might say, get you "SWAG" back. Perhaps 10 to 20 years might have been given away, maybe more! Do you believe you have another 20 or 30 productive years to regain self, self-esteem, self-respect and self-love? Well, I'm not, confessing a God-like control over one's life line, nor am I anyone who gives or takes away life. However, I can only suggest to you, to let *God*, this time, *order your steps* and while he does that, *continually walk in faith.*

Chapter 4

GOD'S INGREDIENTS

Taking back self takes courage, determination and self-love. Understanding how this affects the idea of regaining self will be discussed, here. It's similar to preparing a tasty meal. Special ingredients will add a delicious, tasteful flavor to your palette that will feel good to your mind, body and soul. Let's take a taste of these God-given ingredients. *Taste and see that God is good. (Psalms 34:8)*

COURAGE

Courage is the ability to confront fear, pain, danger, uncertainty, or intimidation. It is having the mental and moral strength to venture, persevere, and withstand danger, fear or difficulty. It is also having the quality of mind and spirit that enables a person to face various adversities.

If you are a giving person, having a mild spirit along with a nurturing personality, people probably view you as being weak, timid, and in plain old words, being a *"push over or a door mat"*, signifying that everyone walks on you or takes advantage of you because you do not defend yourself. Nevertheless, regaining who you truly are and who God made you to be, takes *courage*. Your friends will suddenly realize the change in you and might begin to resent the *"new you, in Christ"*. These friends will turn into being your constituents or counterparts. You will recognize the *"true"* friends by their fruits. Much of what happens from here on, when you give your life to GOD, will not only teach you who you really are, but will also point out who others really are, too.

DETERMINATION

Determination is the ability to decide upon a focus of interest or concern to carry out a particular (focus) in order to achieve a goal, an award, or trustworthy venture. In the famous words of **Colon Powell, United States Ambassador to the United Nations**, he states:

"A dream doesn't become reality through magic,
it takes sweat, determination and hard work"

In *First Corinthians 2:2*, the Apostle Paul, simply sheds light on the concept of determination when he speaks to the congregation in Corinth. He says, *"For I decided to know nothing among you except Jesus Christ and HE who were crucified."* Here, Paul uses the power of having the ability to make a decision leading to a goal. In regaining self, imitate Paul and exercise with strength and determination to stay *focused* on the task ahead in order to become *hold* and *one* with **GOD.**

SELF-LOVE

One should not say they love God and do not love themselves, because God is love and God dwells in you. The gifted and anointed singer, *Whitney Houston,* sang the melodious tune of **"THE GREATEST LOVE OF ALL IS INSIDE OF YOU"**. In regaining self, one of the first and foremost aspects one should recognize is that *courage* and *determination* lies dormant within your soul and spirt, enabling you to make progress and to succeed. When you love yourself, you will find it quite easy to love and to forgive others. Forgiving others as Christ forgives us of our trespasses and sins, is liberating. Since God lives in us, HE already knows the pain we may have experienced and endured as a result of being trespassed against by friends, spouses, children, relatives and others.

Surrendering everything to God will restore courage, determination and self-love back in your life. The GOD in you will empower you with the necessary strength to say **"NO"** without fear, to say **"YES"** with *determination,* to speak with Holy Boldness, with *courage. By* utilizing your newly acquired **"God-given"** strength and power, you will know within your heart and spirit, without a doubt, that your strength comes from on high. Let *Psalms 27* resonate in your spirit. *"The Lord is my strength and my salvation....WHOM SHALL I FEAR."*

Chapter 5

THE DECISION

When a person has been through the *"fire"*, has been burned by the variations of life's experiences and challenges, faced negativity in a marriage or relationship with very few moments of happiness, and, bad days out-weighed good days, that person probably complained. Now, that we have focused on the fact that giving self away to someone or something, other than to God, is **NOT** the best choice, but letting God order your steps and direct your pathway, will always prove to be the *best choice and decision*.

We all live by the decisions we make, such as whether to get a job, where should we live, should we enter a relationship, should we remain single, get married, or if married, should we divorce if the marriage is failing? These decisions can go on and on, forever. The choices we make are not all good or bad. However, making the choice and decision to regain self, is a good decision, especially when you view yourself as your heavenly Father views you.

Making the best decisions can only be made after giving heart-felt thought on how you want to live your life according to how God wants you to live and according to who you are in Christ Jesus. Happiness will be the result when you allow the act of obedience to permeate your thoughts and being. Obedience will cause God to *favor* and *bless* your *new* position in **HIM**.

POSITIONING SELF FOR GOD'S FAVOR

Lavern, an attractive 40 year-old woman, was delighted to have received an invitation to speak at her high school reunion, since she was once elected to be prom queen the year of her high school graduation. In her speech, she related to her colleagues how she struggled to keep her marriage stable, raised four children, and six years after graduating from Lexington High School In Vermont, she decided to go to college to become a Social Worker. Lavern's passion was to be of service to people, especially to women who found themselves on the wrong side of the track, going nowhere. She always availed herself to be of assistants to as many family members, friends and others who were in need of some kind of assistance. Laverne was a help mate to her husband, financially, by obtaining employment in various companies as an office receptionist.

This young woman expressed to her former classmates, that she lost herself along the way, and experienced mental abuse. She also felt that her self-esteem was at an all-time, low. She said she had given herself away, but managed to keep her faith in God and believed God for happiness and the healing of her relationship with her husband, since they were experiencing some difficulties. It was evident to many that her faith in God was steadfast and unmovable.

Lavern learned from her experience that all God wanted her to do was to get in a position where His favor and blessings could rest upon her. She realized that God was not going to bless her while she was in agony and pain or while her self-esteem was so low, nothing could get under it. Realizing this premise, this woman of faith began to position herself so that she could receive the favor of God, and she did.

While sitting by the window one morning watching the neighborhood come to life, cars moving, school busses passing with a lot of sleepy-looking children and watching children running to catch up with friends, laughing and talking, Lavern heard the voice of God. This distinctive voice said to her, "it's time"! The first time she heard those words from the Lord was some years ago and the word, *"time"*, meant it was time to make a mental change, which she did. This time the word *"time"* meant the same thing, only the change must be mental as well as physical. It was *"time"* to get in the position to receive God's favor and blessings.

It may be your time to do something, to act, to move, to live differently, to start a business, change locations, change relationships, or start a new relationship. It may be time to start a new job, leave an old job or change your way of thinking. God blesses those who change according to His will and purposes. He blesses those who change to get their lives in line with HIM, in order that they receive God's Grace. Changing one's position should be taken without fear. However, having some fear is only natural, but having too much fear is not beneficial, but stifling.

A change, if done prayerfully, will give you the strength

and fortitude to proceed. Many, have found themselves lying prostrate before the Lord supplementing for strength and courage to press ahead towards the mark of the high calling. Asking for more faith and trust humbles one to receive supernatural and divine anointing from God.

TAKING BACK

It's mine, shouts a small voice heard in the playground. *"No"*, *"it's not"*, shouts another small voice. Then there were sounds of a struggle, some grunts and moans, indicating that a tug a-war was going on. Finally, one child won and was in possession of the item or thing; in this case, it was a toy. No matter what item it was, the rightful owner, once again, was in possession of it. The little girl had taken back what rightfully belonged to her, and she walked away from her opponent with a smile and a heart full of pride and esteem. That's the same way you should feel when you take back what was taken from you or what you allowed to be stolen from you. Your pride, personality, self-esteem, dignity, education, dreams, talents, hopes and motivation, career aspirations, fiancés, love and your self-worth, should swell up in your soul and spirit, once again.

In another case, let us look at Jackie, an attractive 46-year-old, divorcee with two beautiful children, Eric 14 years old and Renee 12 years old. Let us see how this mother of two children began taking control and claiming her value back—taking back what was stolen from her.

Jackie realized she needed a job to continue her life style after getting through a rough divorce, to adequately care for her two growing children. She realized her skills needed to be upgraded in order to enter the job market once again as a Legal Secretary. Jackie's husband, Charles, who was rather controlling, convinced her that when they got married, 16 years ago, she would not have to work because he wanted her to be a stay-at-home *Mom* when and if children were born into their marriage. He assured her that he would be the only *"bread winner,"* as *head of the household*. This seemed like a good idea, but, Jackie insisted that if they had children, and after the children were old enough to attend school, she would return to work as a Legal Secretary.

As time passed, the couple was blessed with two children. Jackie was a good wife to her husband and an excellent mother to their children. Since Jackie wanted to obey her husband and keep peace in her marriage, she decided to be a stay-at-home Mother, for 17 years. During these years, Jackie gained over 40 pounds, lost her skills and because her husband was so successful, found herself in a position where he always made her feel as though all she was good for was raising the children and being a housewife and maid. Even though there is nothing wrong with being a good mother and wife, her husband began to take advantage of her goodness.

Charles was away from home a lot due to his busy and demanding work schedule and found himself traveling from state-to-state; even at times, to other countries. Although he provided for the family, financially, Jackie deemed that she had lost her identity over the years and felt unfulfilled, and at times, unloved. She felt that her dreams and aspirations were drowned out by Charles' success. She also sensed that her life was put on hold.

It was evident that Jackie loved her family and truly

enjoyed raising her children. Her son Eric was now, 14, ready to enter high school, and her daughter, Renee, was now 16 a high school student hoping to enroll in college upon graduation from high school. Now, Jackie thought, it was time she came out of her shell and passivity, since she realized that although everyone was growing around her, she was at a standstill, helping others to grow, but she was going nowhere. Jackie returned to college, upgraded her skills, received a Bachelor's Degree in Business, and is now working for a prestigious law firm as a high-powered Partner's Legal Administrator. She is doing exceptionally well, financially. Her life has changed, since she took back what she allowed others to take from her own life.

Jackie's husband, Charles, divorced her after having an affair with one of his co-workers. He is now living in another state. Although this was an exhausting and painful experience, Jackie and her children are holding on to God's unchanging hand, and all of them are doing well.

Have you ever been in a situation like Jackie? Perhaps you might know someone in a similar predicament and is striving to come out of it. Some men and women have been successful, while others are yet struggling to achieve and regain their identity, purpose, usefulness, dignity, courage, self-worth and self-esteem. There is no magic in this achievement! Applying the ingredients of faith, determination, courage, self-love and prayer, with God's guidance, a successful transition will be obtained. *Deliver me in thy righteousness, incline thine ear unto me and save me. (Psalms 71:2)*

Chapter 6

LIGHTS, CAMERA, ACTION

In your mind, you are probably asking yourself this question, *"HOW"* does one regain self without retaliating with revenge and ager, if those attributes are experienced in one's mind? Christians, too, are challenged and angered as was Christ's disciple, Simon, Peter. *"Then Simon Peter having a sword drew it and struck the high priest's servant and cut off his right ear. The servant's name was Malchus." (John 18:10)* How many Malchus' do we have in our lives? How many did we have in our lives? If they are still there, what action is needed, now that the *spotlight* is on **YOU,** since it's your time to take your bow and shine like a budding new star in God's army?

Action means, that something has to be done in order to achieve the desired results. In this case, one's mind must be prepared for the action taken, to be successful. In doing so, ask God to release all fears and restore holy boldness back in your life and spirit. What is holy boldness? It is simply speaking and thinking with the mind of Christ. That is, with wisdom, love and peace being in the forefront. Keeping in mind Psalms 19:4, *"Let the words of my mouth and the mediation of my heart, be acceptable in thy sight, oh Lord, my strength and my redeemer"*. Acquiring holy boldness will help you to rely on God for strength, acknowledging that **HE** is your key to redemption—restoring you and allowing you to take b back what the enemy has stolen, destroyed and robbed from you. Let God, this time, be in total control, and not you. *Why?* We are only flesh and blood, with sinful inclinations and might allow ourselves to become remorseful, angry, depressed, revengeful, and even suicidal. In Ephesians 4:26, Paul recognized that we as humans have the capacity and freedom to be angry; it is an emotional response that is innate, but controllable. He was inspired of God to write, *"Don't sin by letting anger control you." Don't let the sun go down while you are still, angry." (Ephesians 4:26 - 27)*

An essential action in order to shine like a budding new star in God's army is to *FORGIVE*. That is, to renounce anger or resentment against someone or a thing. The act of forgiveness will prevent you from imposing punishment on the offender. In this case, the offender is the one whom **YOU** allowed yourself to be given to, other than to GOD. Many people have made remarks such as, "it's hard to forgive", or "I can't forgive because I'm still hurting", I can't forgive because they didn't say that they were sorry". Sounds familiar? Of course! However, if we just think about how God has forgiven ALL OF US over and over, then we should forgive our trespassers as they forgive us. Jesus suffered and died for OUR sins and INQUITIES, so we ought to forgive others.

The last action before taking our *"BOW"* as the curtain to a new life opens, is to find it in *our* heart to *FORGIVE* ourselves. Self-forgiveness will open the door to unlimited opportunities, leading to self-improvement, spiritual blessings, along with Godly empowerment. The scripture states, whom God frees, are free indeed. Freedom, like forgiveness, is a gift God gives. Any gift given, especially divinely, is to be cherished along with a great amount of appreciation and respect. Utilizing this gift to edify and magnify God, thus, bestowing the power of forgiveness on others, by exercising the **ACTION,** you are allowing someone to glorify our GOD.

TAKE YOUR FINAL BOW

As the curtain opens to a new life for you, take your final *"Bow"* to the Master designer of ALL creation, "GOD". In this *Bow* thank **HIM** for enlightening the pathway to spiritual, physical, mental and social success and empowerment. In this empowerment, your self-esteem is elevated. Fear and other inadequacies are eliminated. Doubts and purposelessness are vanished. Love of self is restored. Now is the time to re-acquaint yourself with who you are, and who you are in Christ, Jesus. Take time for yourself, again. Be concerned about your physical appearance and begin to care for yourself, again. In other words, love yourself as God loves you.

Take a glimpse of what your life would look like when you re-discover self and embrace the power that was given to you from the very beginning of your existence, before you unknowingly, gave yourself away to someone other than to GOD. You will rejoice to find yourself, again, while still loving your husband, children, extended family, co-workers, friends and others.

Now, go forth, says the Lord, empowered and

blessed. Go forth with knowledge, understanding truth and wisdom. Proving yourselves acceptable as a child of God by utilizing the power within to give yourselves to **GOD ONLY.** This empowerment will enable you to carry out God's will for your life, in an effectual and intelligent manner as children of the **KING.**

My fervent prayer is for *all* to reap the many blessings God has in store for *all*, now and in the blessed days to come, remembering God's admonishment in the book of *Proverbs 4:20 – 22 "My son attend to thy words, incline thine ear unto my sayings, let them not depart from thine eyes; keep them in the midst of thine heart, for they are life to all who find them and health for the whole body."* Be confident in your present and future and trust in the words mentioned in *Hebrews 10:35* where the Apostle, Paul, states: *"I do not fling away my fearless confidence, for it carries a great and glorious compensation of reward."*

In conclusion, by the power of God that is invested in us, we are equipped and covered by the Grace of God. We can now put all of our trust in HIM, not Giving Ourselves Away, But to HIM, Only, becoming more than conquerors as we continue to serve HIM in truth, knowledge and wisdom. By doing this, we gain HIS amazing grace and approval, therefore, giving **ALL HONOR** and **PRAISES** to our *Awesome GOD,* **IN THE PRECIOUS NAME OF HIS SON, JESUS CHRIST.**

"Now unto HIM that is able
To keep you from falling,
And to present you faultless
Before the presence of HIS Glory
With exceeding joy,
To the only wise GOD our Savior,
Be Glory and Majesty,
Dominion and Power,
Both Now and Forever - AMEN"